The Death of Socrates

The Death of Socrates

Narrated by
Jean Paul Mongin

Illustrated by
Yann Le Bras

Translated by
Anna Street

Plato & Co.
diaphanes

Tell us, Delphic Oracle, who is the wisest man in Greece?

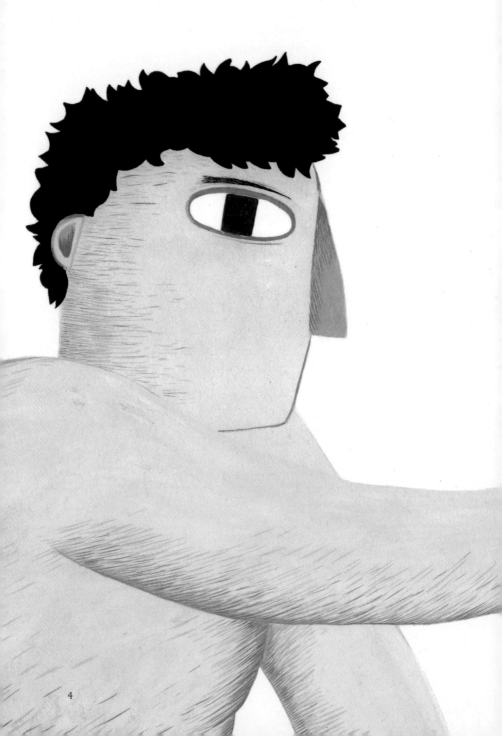

"In Greece as in all the rest of the world," replied the Oracle, "no mortal is wiser than Socrates, for Socrates is in love with the truth."

Socrates invites people to know themselves.
He walks the roads of Athens, calling out to
whomever he finds on his path.

"Hello you there, the finest of men, citizen of Athens, the greatest city of all! You worry about honors, your reputation, pleasures and your fortune! But do you also think about seeking the truth, making your soul wiser, in short, about practicing philosophy?"

When the persons to whom he talks take themselves to be very wise, Socrates plays around with them by asking so many questions that they end up admitting their ignorance. When he runs into ignorant people, Socrates sets them on the way to wisdom.
Socrates himself claims to know only one single thing: that he knows nothing at all!

By constantly philosophizing and asking everyone questions, interrogating scholars on their knowledge and uncovering their ignorance, Socrates ends up making a lot of people very angry. Those who brag about their knowledge hate him most of all.

They call him Socrates the Talkative Tramp, and decide to take legal proceedings against him. In front of the Athenian Assembly, they accuse him of corrupting the young and of not honoring the gods.
Socrates speaks in his defense...

"People of Athens! It is said that I dream of the celestial bodies, that I scrutinize the things under the earth and teach the young a bunch of balderdash about all of this. Aristophanes even wrote a comedy, in which a certain Socrates walks around on stage, floats into the air and rambles on with questions about which I know nothing!

But the truth is that I have never pretended to educate young
people! For were it a matter of breeding colts, or baby calves,
I would know exactly whom to ask. But as for educating children,
in order to make them into men and citizens, one needs knowledge
that I do not possess, I who know nothing."

Big Meletus, who wants to see Socrates dead, tries to put him on the spot:

"But Socrates," he calls out in his falsetto voice, "if you're not trying to educate, what is it that you do all day? If there is nothing unusual about your goings-on, why are you being criticized?"

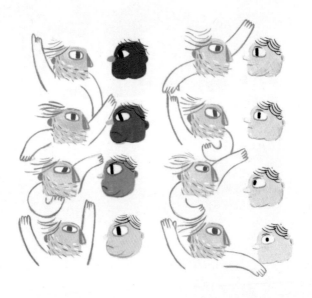

"Meletus," replies Socrates, "and you, are you saying that I corrupt the young?"

"That is what I claim most emphatically!"

"Are you dragging me before the courts because I corrupt the young intentionally or do I do so unintentionally?"

"Intentionally, of course!"

"But tell us, illustrious Meletus, is it better to live in a city of decent people, or in a city of malicious people?"

"In a city of fine people, most certainly."

"Would I then be so crazy as to wish to live among those who would do me harm?" continues Socrates, imitating his accuser's squeaky voice.

"No, of course not! But I accuse you of teaching new deities!" Meletus yelps, furious. "Because you, you do not believe in the gods! You even say that the sun and the moon are not gods, but a rock and an earth!"

"It is Anaxagoras, my dear man, and not I, who teaches these strange doctrines. But answer me this: how can I introduce new deities if I do not even believe in the gods?" asks Socrates.

Meletus, infuriated, does not reply.

"Athenians, my friends," announces Socrates, bowing slightly,
"I salute you! You can see that the accusations brought against
me are worthless!

To tell the truth, it is the gods themselves who have sent me
to awaken our City! So day after day and wherever I might be,
I badger you, I criticize you for seeking after riches rather than truth.

I am like a big mosquito pestering a large horse in order to sting it and prevent it from dozing off. Perhaps out of irritation, you would like to get rid of me and sleep for the rest of your life...

Yet such is the task the gods have assigned to me! Must I then cease to practice philosophy, to invite those I encounter to love truth over appearances? It would be impious to forsake my calling for fear of death! Athenians, I will continue to question my fellow men, even if I must be condemned for it 100 times over!"

In the assembly, a rumbling starts to rise: among the judges, some find Socrates lacking in respect. Others admire his courage.

"It is true," continues Socrates, "that I stick my nose in everyone else's business, but that doesn't mean I am pretending to govern the City!

You see, ever since my childhood, a kind of little demon, or a divine genie, prevents me from getting into mischief; and this genie tells me that I wouldn't live very long if I got involved in politics!

Remember the time I found myself by chance presiding over this Council. On that day, you wanted to illegally judge the ten generals who had failed to collect the bodies of our soldiers after the battle of Arginusae. Alone against all, I pointed out that the law does not allow several citizens to be tried at the same time. You almost massacred me along with them!

In my opinion, when one gets involved in politics and fights for justice, one does not wish to live to a ripe old age!
My little demon preserves me from this!

The truth, you see, Athenians, is that I have never given in to injustice. Meletus says that I corrupt my students; yet I am no one's teacher! If someone likes to listen to me when I speak, then whether he be old or young, rich or poor, I never send him away, nor do I ask him for anything. But if afterwards he becomes good or bad, for this I am not responsible!

Come on, men of Athens! For lesser things, other defendants entreat you with pleas. They sob and try to arouse your pity by bringing their small children to give testimony. I will do nothing of the sort for that is not worthy of our City, or of the wise man's reputation that has been ascribed to me. Such a show displeases the gods. Since I am accused of not honoring them, well fine! I appeal to them to judge me."

The assembly of the Five Hundred, which judges Socrates, votes: Socrates is declared guilty, by a thirty-vote margin. Athenian custom demands that the two sides must then recommend a punishment: the accusers usually ask for a tough penalty, and the accused for a similar but lighter penalty. The judges then choose which sanction seems the most appropriate to them. Unsurprisingly, big Meletus and his group of false scholars called for Socrates to be put to death. It is now up to Socrates, who appears to be enjoying himself, to recommend a sentence. He is expected to suggest exile.

"What is the penalty, citizen judges, a man like me deserves, whose only wrong is not to lead a peaceful life minding his own business? A man who seeks the good rather than riches? Who prefers the City itself to its honors? What punishment should be reserved for this poor wise man who needs to be taken care of in order to continue his good deeds?

Athenians, here is the penalty I deserve: put me up, at your expense, in the beautiful palace of Prytaneion where you house the champions of the Olympic Games and your most distinguished guests."

A loud clamor broke out in the assembly: what insolence! This is too much! Socrates is then condemned to die by drinking a cup of poison hemlock.

"My little demon would warn me if I should fear any evil,"
quietly stated Socrates to his devastated friends; "but death is
either nothing, or else it is the soul's journey to another place.

If death is nothing, it is like a dreamless sleep, such as on one
of these beautiful nights, more peaceful than all our days:
what a marvelous gain!

And if death is, as they say, a crossing over to the Underworld;
if I can meet Homer, Hesiod and Orpheus there, the poets of old,
and the greatest heroes, Ajax, Odysseus; if I can interrogate the
wisdom of thousands of men who have gone before without risking
condemnation, what greater blessing could there be?

All the same, dear friends, now it is time for us to part ways,
I to die and you to live. Which of us has the happier prospect?
Only the gods know!"

At this time of the year, however, Athens is on holiday, celebrating the voyage of the prince Theseus, who, in ancient times, set out to kill the Minotaur in order to break the yoke that the appalling Minos, the king of Crete, had laid upon the City. It is the custom that no execution should take place before a ship sails to Crete and returns. Socrates thus remains an entire month in prison, where he writes songs.

IN ETERNAL CONFLICT, JOY AND PAIN,
GOD WISHED TO RECONCILE THEM.
IT DIDN'T WORK, SO HE TOOK THEM
AND TIED THEM TO EACH OTHER.
AND EVER SINCE YOU CAN BE SURE
WHEN ONE OF THEM BEFALLS
THE OTHER IS NOT FAR BEHIND
BUT FOLLOWS CLOSE THE CALL.

One day, early in the morning, Socrates awakens in his cell to find his friend Crito beside him.

"What are you doing here so early?" he asks sleepily.

"I am admiring you," replies Crito, "how you sleep so peacefully whereas fate has dealt with you so harshly! As for me, what dismal news I have to announce!"

"Has the ship returning from Crete entered the harbor, ending the festival period?"

"No, but its arrival is said to be imminent," murmurs Crito.

"I was just dreaming," replies Socrates, "that a woman full of grace, dressed in white, was speaking to me in the words of king Agamemnon to the hero Achilles. 'Socrates,' she said, 'in three days, you will reach your fertile homeland...'"

"What a strange dream, Socrates!"

"What a clear omen, rather!"

"Socrates, my friend, I beg of you, allow us to arrange for your escape! I can easily bribe the prison guards. A small boat awaits to transport you to safety, and friends will welcome you everywhere you go.

If you refuse to do this for yourself, do it for your sons, so they will not have to live as orphans! Do it for us, so it will not be said that we left you to perish even though we could have saved you!"

"Who cares what might be said?" yawns Socrates. "What do I care about dying? The important thing is not simply to live, but to live well, that is to say, to live justly, don't you think so?"

"Yes, Socrates, we have already agreed upon this subject."

"Is it sometimes just, nevertheless, to commit an injustice? To repay injustice with injustice, for example? Or indeed is injustice never fair or good?"

"Injustice is always a bad thing, that's for sure."

"Well then, tell me, my dear Crito: would it be just to bribe the guards and to escape, even though the Athenians have not liberated me? Take a look! My little demon acts the Law of Athens for us!"

"Socrates, you like asking questions;
I, in turn, will interrogate you.

It is I, the Law of Athens, who authorized the
marriage of your parents, again I who protected
your childhood, I who determine your life in
the City.

I am more than a mother or a father to you.
Do you so despise me that you try to escape
from me?

Your duty, is it not to obey me, to hold the
position I order you to take, as you did during
the war when fighting in my name?"

"You see, Crito," resumes Socrates, *"I like living by the Law of Athens so much that I refused, during my trial, to consider exile. And all that to now break this Law by escaping? To disguise myself as a slave, and to run off with my children, in order to turn them into foreigners? Or abandon them here? Would I ever again dare speak to men, as I have up until now, to tell them that nothing is more valuable than virtue, justice, the Law?"*

Crito leaves the prison, and announces Socrates' resolution to his friends. The next day, the ship returning from Crete enters the Athenian harbor, and the festival period comes to an end.

The day has come on which the sentence must be carried out. All of Socrates' friends have gathered to be near him: Crito and his son Critobulus, Hermogenes, Epigenes, Aeschines, Phaedo, Antisthenes, Ctesippus of Peania, Menexenus, Cebes, Simmias of Thebes, and many others as well. The only one missing is Plato, who is unwell. Unwell? A cold, probably.

Inside the prison, Socrates is with his wife Xanthippe and their youngest child, Sophronicus. Xanthippe, who is ordinarily bad-tempered, is moaning and wailing all the time:

"Oh! Socrates! Behold your friends, it is the last time you can speak to them!"

Socrates asks Crito to take his wife home. While she is being led away, Xanthippe cries out and tears at her hair.

As for Socrates, he is just as he always is; scratching his legs, playing with words, speaking of his little demon and philosophizing with his friends. Simmias of Thebes asks him why he is not sad to have to die.

"My good Simmias," replies Socrates, "I am going to try and answer you, and to be more persuasive than I was during my trial! To be honest, I wouldn't be so content to be taking this trip to the Underworld if I weren't convinced that I will find other gods there that are absolutely good, and perhaps men even better than those from here. And then admit that it would be funny, after having spent my life practicing philosophy, which is to say a certain way of practicing death, to go and run away from it as I run away from my wife, whereas this death sets me free of her!"

"Socrates, you still make me laugh, even if my heart's not in it!" Simmias guffaws. "Thus, in saying that you deserve death, your judges judged right after all!"

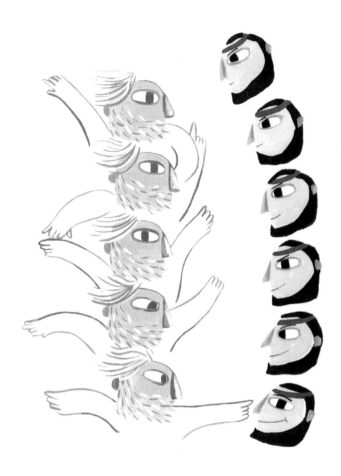

"In a way, yes," Socrates smiles, "apart from the fact that they don't see death as I do! But leave my judges alone!"

Then Simmias tunes his lyre in order to accompany
Socrates as he recites a poem:

"When the swan feels the end is nigh
It hails the gods with an unknown tune.
Weak men, who are afraid to die,
Slander the beast, calling it moved,
By a deep sorrow, which its singing
Expresses to the world as it is leaving.
But does a bird sing for sadness?
Neither the nightingale, nor the hummingbird
The soul of the swan, in the eyes of Hades
Recognizes its true homeland
The Bird of Apollo can fathom in its mind
The marvels that lay in store for its kind
And I, like the swan, do celebrate
The good things that after this life me await"

"When a man dies," asks Socrates afterwards, "does something happen?"

"Uh well . . . yes," replies Simmias, laying down his lyre.

"What happens is that the body and the soul take leave of each other, isn't that right?"

"Absolutely," says Simmias.

"Pay close attention now," continues Socrates: "do you believe that what is called a philosopher, a man who loves wisdom, is very concerned with his pleasures, for example, with what he might eat or drink?"

"Not at all, Socrates!"

"And what about love's pleasures, caring for his body, or the color of his shoes? Do you think that a philosopher worries about these things, beyond what is strictly necessary?"

"If he attends to those things, then he is not a genuine philosopher," Simmias asserts.

"My good Simmias, we are in agreement: a philosopher hardly attends to bodily pleasures, but to those of the soul. Let us go even further: are we not occasionally mistaken as to what we see or hear?"

"Indeed, that happens!"

"So," Socrates says, *"the body can be a source of error for the soul, which is why the philosopher prefers to reason and seek after truth in itself. In the same way, for example, would you say that justice is something or that it is nothing?"*

"Something, definitely."

"And would you say as much of the good and the beautiful?"

"How could I deny it?"

"But have you ever seen justice, the good or the beautiful, or even greatness with your own eyes?"

"No," replies Simmias. "I have seen things that were just, beautiful or great. But as for justice itself, beauty itself, greatness itself, I have never seen them."

"It is therefore not by our body that we know these realities, but by our soul. And we know them all the better if we are less disturbed by our body!"

"Socrates, nobody could have said it better!"

"As long as my soul remains chained to my body, I will never possess the wisdom that I love. I must constantly take care of my body; on top of that, it gets sick and disturbs my soul with desires, fears, passions, in short, all sorts of foolishness, without mentioning quarrels, and the wars that follow. In order to become wise, the soul must take leave of the body, and contemplate the reality of things on its own. Do you not think so, Simmias?"

"Yes, Socrates, absolutely!"

"It is thus after my death, once my soul and body are separated, that I have hope of encountering the wisdom with which I am so in love. How could I be sad to die, my dear Simmias?"

"That would indeed be, quite thoughtless, Socrates!"

"As for what will happen to my soul after the death of my body to which it is bound, I will tell you what I think...

When at death, the soul separates from the body, the little demon,
the divine genie, which was its guardian, takes it by the hand
and leads it along the twisted and narrow paths that lead to the
Underworld. The soul of the unreasonable man cannot resign itself
to leave his body, and its little demon has a difficult time pulling it
along the path. When it arrives, completely furious, to the place it
was meant to be, it frightens all the other souls, and from then on,
spends its time wandering, troubled and alone.

On the other hand, the soul of the wise man, which during his life has been purified by philosophy, makes this journey without mishap. The souls of the other wise men wait for it at the end, and all of them sit together next to the gods, in one of the earth's marvelous places.

For the earth is very big, and we know only this little part along the sea between the river Phasis and the Pillars of Hercules; numerous peoples live in other, unknown regions. We think we walk upon the surface of the earth in bright daylight, but in fact, we live deep inside vast, dark caves, into which the rains pour.

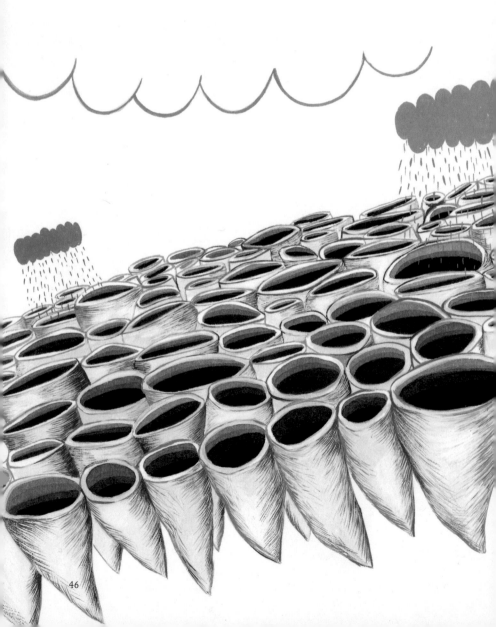

Imagine those who live in the depths of the sea. Through the water, they catch glimpses of the sun and the stars, and they mistake the surface of the ocean for the sky. In the same way, we call the air heaven, since it is where we observe the path of the stars.

Yet if a man from the depths of the seas could raise himself up to us, he would see how much the world from whence he came is full of sand and sludge, rocky and worn away by the salt. And if we ourselves, we could rise up and leave our cave, and walk out onto the true earth, we would gaze at a light incomparable to ours, and other even greater marvels.

This real earth above us resembles a multi-colored striped balloon, of which the artists' palette down here is only a pale reflection: one part is a phenomenal purple, another is a white brighter than snow, yet another is tinted gold of an unknown purity.

Deep inside our cave, the shadows and the darkness cloud the colors, whereas above they are pure. The mountains there are all made of precious stones, of which only a few fragments fall down to where we are. Both the animals and the men there are free from disease, and they live very long and very happy lives.

The keenness of hearing, sight and
understanding of the inhabitants of this land above
is as superior to ours as air is purer and lighter than water.
They see the sun, the moon and the stars as they really are.
Their temples are truly inhabited by gods, who speak to men
as I am speaking to you. Such is the true earth above us.

Around the earth, there are numerous caves like the one in which
we find ourselves. Some are bigger than ours, and let in more light.
Others are deeper or darker. All these caves are pierced with holes,
which join them together. Often rivers of hot or cold waters, of
mud more or less thick, of fire and of lava pour into these holes
and come out somewhere else, through springs or volcanoes.
These rivers merge together near the deepest cave of all, which
 the poets name the Tartarus, where they flow with a terrible roar.

51

Most men, whose souls are neither really wise nor really bad, are led after their deaths to the edge of the grim river Acheron by their little demon. That is where they meet up with their fellow creatures and climb aboard a small craft which transports them through desert regions, following an underground course, all the way to the Acherusian marsh. There they stay for a certain time, in order to purify themselves, then they are sent back to be reborn among the living. The criminal souls of those who raided temples or treated their parents with violence are thrown into the Tartarus. A river of fire called Phlegethon carries them away, and the most wicked never come back. However, among them are souls which are capable of being cleansed, for example those of criminals who had acted out of anger and felt remorse all their life. Those souls, after a very long time, are thrown back into the Cocytus river, which runs along the Acherusian marsh: as they pass by, they catch a glimpse of the souls of those they have wronged, and they beg them to be allowed to come out of the river. If the victims of their injustices have pity on them, they can reunite, and their torments are over. If not, they return for a stay in the roar of Tartarus, then set off again on the river, and so on until they have convinced those whom they have mistreated to welcome them.

As for the men who have lived holy lives, their little demon does not lead them towards the rivers to be carried into the depths. When they die, they ascend towards the true earth and its marvels. And among them, those who have been entirely purified by philosophy then live absolutely without a body, in dwellings even more beautiful than the others.

You see, my friends, how much wisdom is worth seeking.
The reward for it is great! That said, you must excuse me,
but I do not want to leave my wife the burden of washing a corpse:
it is time for me to take a bath!"

"Socrates, don't leave like this!" cries out Criton. "Tell us what
you would like us to do after your death, for your children or
for whomever you would like!"

"What I would like you to do? Only that which I have always
told you: seek after wisdom, do not be concerned with the pleasures
of the body or its clothing."

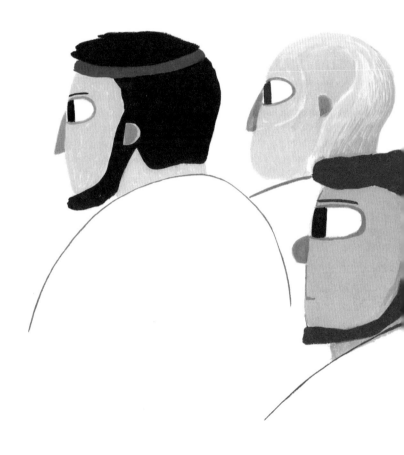

"At least tell us how you would like to be buried!"

"As you would like! But you'll have to catch me first!"
Socrates replies with a soft laugh.

Socrates goes to take his bath, then his children are brought to him. Two are very young, their names are Sophroniscus and Menexenus. The oldest is named Lamprocles. Socrates embraces them, gives them instructions, and sends them away. The sun is already setting.

A prison guard brings a cup filled with hemlock:

"Drink, Socrates! And then walk around the room so that the poison will take effect more quickly. When you feel your legs getting heavy, lie down."

Socrates raises his cup and declares:

"Here's to the gods! May they keep watch over my journey!"

Then he drinks in one gulp, and his friends start weeping, feeling less sorry for Socrates than for themselves, so soon to be deprived of such a companion!

"Do stop your lamentations, have you gone insane?" Socrates scolds. *"I didn't send away the women so that my friends would start up a similar spectacle! Come on! Be calm, be strong!"*

He continues walking around the room; his legs become heavy, he lies down and covers his head. The man who brought the hemlock tests his feet, asking Socrates if he can feel them. Socrates motions that he cannot. In this manner, the man moves up the length of his legs, which are becoming stiff and cold, as the poison spreads. When Socrates' stomach becomes cold, he lifts the piece of tunic from his face and says softly:

"Crito, we owe Asclepius, the god of medicine, the sacrifice of a cock!"

Then Socrates falls quiet. And so dies the man the Athenians condemned for not having honored the gods.

French edition
Jean Paul Mongin & Yann Le Bras:
La mort du divin Socrate
Design: Yohanna Nguyen
© Les petits Platons, Paris 2012

First edition
ISBN 978-3-03734-544-3
© diaphanes, Zurich-Berlin 2015

www.platoandco.net
www.diaphanes.com

Layout: 2edit, Zurich
Printed and bound in Germany